WHAT OTI

The Handbook for In

———— ❦ ————

"You're like a superhero author,
saving one relationship at a time!"

~Tekayla, recent college graduate, single

"The antidote to most of the rubbish promoted as 'science.'"

~Jim D., married 30 years, father of 3

"This book is the prerequisite to
successful relationships and marriages."

~Debbie T., married, 3 kids

"Wow, what an unexpected journey.
The grocery list—something I needed to read.
This is not only well-developed but also timely."

~Scott E., middle-aged, single

"I like the all-around lovely idea of a relationship IQ.
This is a warm-hearted and supportive gesture
for your fellow man and woman."

~Andrew W., college student, single

"While you address difficult problem areas, you make it sound
easy and convincing that they can be overcome with a little
honesty and openness. I found your approach thought-provoking,
knowledgeable, and dignified. Pity, not everybody knows how
to write a shopping list, because it would be so good. Using
your terminology, I find that most people would rather go to the
supermarket and throw everything possible (and affordable)
into their trolley, only to chuck it in the bin when it's not really
wanted on inspection. (The scarf is a winner.)"

~Almuth W., married, 6 children

The Handbook for Increasing Your Relationship IQ

THE HANDBOOK FOR

INCREASING YOUR
RELATIONSHIP IQ

EDWARD L. FAIRLEY

Langdon Street Press

Langdon Street Press
212 3rd Avenue North, Suite 290
Minneapolis, MN 55401
612.455.2293
www.langdonstreetpress.com

ISBN-13: 978-1-936183-81-4
LCCN: 2010939175

Cover Design and Typeset by Madge Duffy

Printed in the United States of America

CONTENTS

This book is dedicated to those who are looking for love's clarity and understanding.

FOREWORD

———— ⚜ ————

In retrospect, I lived in what now seems like a life of silence for too many years. There were many years where I felt that my own was the only audible voice heard, as if I were singing a solo when the world needed to hear a choir. Not until I received an unexpected phone call from a friend I hadn't spoken to in more than three years, did I feel I finally *heard* from someone who knew the words to the song I had been trying to sing. After years of knowing my friend Eddie, it wasn't until this day that I finally knew someone who could actually teach me the words to the song I used to hum my way through.

The day I received that phone call from my friend is one I will not soon forget. In one minute, I was filled with surprise to receive the call and also with pride to answer the question about what I had been up to. Amazingly, we had been doing the same thing— writing books. After going into more depth about the books we were writing, I began to doubt that he made the right choice in the book he chose to write. I didn't question or doubt his talent or intellect; I just had never conversed with him on the topic of relationships. I couldn't help but think how hard it would be for him to market this book, being he is not famous, or a recognized authority, or an expert on the topic of relationships. I quickly accepted his offer to read what my friend had written, but I questioned whether I was reading it only with the hope of enjoying it, or if I wanted to confirm my initial thinking that he had no business writing such a book.

In the end, I was not only happy to have read this book, but I have been truly blessed by its practical power. I finally found the missing words to the song I'd been humming for a lifetime. *The Handbook* spoke to me like a well-written sermon. My friend wrote this relationship book in a voice that can be understood by any type of person: educated, uneducated, young, old, married, or single. The writing is engaging as well as inspiring. *The Handbook* compels you to analyze your past and current relationships. Eddie speaks to the needs and the lack of awareness in relationships in such a way that, before you finish the first chapter, you forget that he is not a recognized relationship authority (yet) and become grateful that he decided to share.

You will soon see that all people were created for a purpose and, even if you have yet to realize your own, it will be clear to you that Brother Eddie is walking, or should I say writing, in his. I feel that this is a cosign-able piece, meaning: I cosign and endorse the greatness of this wisdom, in hopes that people will remember me as the one who referred it to them, for it will make them appreciate me more because I had the good sense to recognize its wisdom. Enjoy!

~ J. L. Lewis, author of *How Much More You Need*

INTRODUCTION

According to Robert Grazian in 2009, forty-to-fifty percent of first-time marriages end in divorce. Sixty-to-seventy percent of second and third marriages end in divorce. The top-five causes for these are poor communication, financial problems, lack of commitment to the marriage, dramatic changes in priorities, and infidelity. Though I'm not a fan of statistics, I bring them to your attention because, after reading this book, you will know better how to avoid these issues.

I am not a marriage counselor or a psychiatrist; nor do I consider myself a professional, expert, or a guru on the subject of relationships. I am simply a man with an ongoing interest in analyzing relationship experiences (my own and others). This has no doubt been influenced by the fact that my two older sisters and I were raised by a single mother who knew her share of conflict in relationships. She moved us out of the country when I was seven to get away from my father, who had some years before tried to kill her and was soon to be released from prison. We had a hard life for a time in Haiti. That is history now and my father turned his life around and became a respected pastor. But along the way I became sensitized to many of the factors that cause relationships to fail. Oftentimes it's the simple, most obvious things that we overlook when it comes to problems or relationship issues. That's why we overlook them.

My goals in writing this book are: first; to expose the unhelpful myths about males and females that society, your family, and other biased authors have injected into your mind; and second, to shed light on the simple things that cause relationships to be unsuccessful. This will help you identify some of the causes of past relationship failures, perhaps even save your current relationships, or help you prevent these things from happening in your future relationships. My third goal is to describe common situations that cause people to have problems in their marriages. Finally, I will focus on what causes marriages and relationships to become stale and boring, while also providing you with ways to keep your relationship/marriage fresh and new.

CHAPTER I

———— ❧ ————

Detoxification

The first step in increasing your relationship intelligence quotient (IQ) is to detoxify yourself of the myths that society and our culture have injected into your mind about how all males and females should or do think and act. The same way you can't use the views and actions of one person or a few persons of a particular race to represent the views and actions of an entire race, you can't use the views and actions of one person or a few persons to represent the views and actions of a particular gender. It frustrates me to see book titles such as *Men Are From Mars, Women Are From Venus, Understanding Women, Everything You Need To Know About Men... You Can Learn From Dogs,* or to hear a man offhandedly remark to his son or a young boy, "All these women in the house and there's nothing cooked." These are examples of how people categorize the roles of males and females, or draw a mental picture of how men or women *should* act.

God has made us all different individuals, and to be aware of this and still generalize about the behavior of men or women is inappropriate. Clearly all women aren't the same, nor are all men. Yet society, our families, friends, pastors, teachers, the Internet, authors, and the media consistently tell or show us what kind of characteristics men and women have, and how the two sexes react emotionally to various situations. We take those messages and run with them, even teach them to our children. I agree that prior to the mid-to-late nineteenth century, when "horse power" really meant horse power since people traveled by horse, and the man was typically the sole provider of the family, he expected to come home to a meal and a clean house. I believe that how clean the house *should* be kept depends upon the ages and number of children a particular couple has to care for. Taking care of children is no easy task. Keep in mind, there were times when women were rarely allowed to work outside the home, and they were raised and instructed to play the primary role in taking care of their children and in carrying out the household chores.

Now let us fast forward to the reality of now. In most cases, men are no longer the sole providers of the household, nor do we depend on riding horses for transportation. Women now hold high-powered positions and are faced with the same future expectations as men. **Times have changed.** With time, we change our views of technology, education, fashion, and the way we raise our children but, for some reason, we hold stagnantly to outdated roles of men and women. We've got to change this mindset. Most families need more than one income to support a family; this is why, in most households, both parents work outside of the home, often full time.

Women work to provide for and help with the responsibilities of a household (i.e., cleaning, cooking, taking care of the children and the vehicles, etc). Notice I said *help*; this responsibility should be shared 100/100, not 50/50. Never give your spouse, or anyone you share yourself with, half of yourself. Not to mention, it would behoove every person to be well versed in all of the household and vehicle duties. The reason for this, other than genuinely wanting to be helpful to your partner, is this reality: if and when your spouse or other "whole" is incapacitated or no longer around (be it from sickness, death, or divorce), those responsibilities will still be there. So it makes sense to be proactive and be prepared for that now. It is imperative that you never assume that, just because a person is a certain gender, they *will* act or *should* act in a certain manner.

The only way to understand a person fully is over time and by engaging in ongoing communication with that individual. Realize that all people are unique and different, and you will be well on your way to increasing your relationship IQ.

CHAPTER II

---- ✤ ----

The Less You Give, the More You Receive

The second step in increasing your relationship IQ is to, when dating, give less so you will receive more. I'm aware that this sounds unorthodox, so allow me to draw you a picture to help you see what I mean by this statement.

Imagine a Hawaiian surfer who, while enjoying the best wave she ever rode, suffered a cramp, fell off her surfboard, drowned, and passed away. After passing away, she immediately arrives at heaven's gates. She's met by God who provides her with a proposition: before entering heaven, she must first make two copies of a list of her favorite colors and hobbies, then spend a day in heaven and hell, and finally decide where she wanted to spend eternity.

The surfer enjoyed making the two copies of her list of favorite colors and hobbies. It helped her reminisce about being home and surfing the waves. It wasn't long before she handed God the two copies and began day one, in heaven.

The surfer walked through the pearly gates where she was met by an angel. The angel provided her with a halo, some wings, a harp that played with no need of her being skilled (for it played itself), and a king-sized cloud for comfort when she rested. Her day consisted of floating through heaven on her cloud while passing other angels who did the same, and listening to her harp that played classical music.

At day's end, the surfer arrived on her cloud at God's throne. God informed her that she had concluded her day, and it was time for her twenty-four-hour tour of hell. She proceeded to the elevator that God directed her to, and pressed the down button.

The elevator door opened in hell and she couldn't believe her eyes. She was amidst a heavenly snapshot of Hawaii...sand, palm trees, and waves that were miles long. Right at her feet next to a palm tree, standing out of the sand, was a surfboard tailor-made for her body. This surfboard contained all of her favorite colors with her name engraved on it. She hugged the surfboard and smiled, almost cried. She was then accompanied by other surfers, and they surfed the whole day. The day ended so quickly that she thought to herself, *Time goes by fast when you're having fun.*

The surfer was politely escorted back to the elevator by the friendly people she surfed with. She was reluctant to press the up button, thinking to herself that she was not yet ready to stand before God to make such a hard decision. It seemed as if the door opened as soon as she hit the up button. There was God, not wasting any time. He immediately asked where she decided to spend eternity.

She nervously replied, "God, I never thought I'd say this, but I think I'd rather spend my eternity in hell."

God seemed sad, but again directed her to the elevator where she pressed the down button. She felt bad for making God sad, but when the elevator door closed and she thought about where she was headed, she got excited and forgot all about it. Her excitement and anticipation made the elevator ride seem extremely slow this time, but she finally arrived.

Again, when the doors opened, she couldn't believe her eyes. Where was once beautiful sand, now was coal and trash. The beautiful waves were now volcanic lava; the palm trees were extinct, and the people were dirty with third-degree burns all over their bodies. She dropped to her knees and began to cry. The devil arrived with a familiar list in his hand. She looked up and asked what happened to the sand, palm trees, beautiful people, and incredible waves. The devil replied, while smiling at the second copy of her list of favorite colors and hobbies, "When you visited the first time I was an agent recruiting you into my establishment. Now I own you and I can be myself."

In this story, God and the devil knew everything there was to know about the Hawaiian surfer woman. God didn't feel the need to adjust who he was to express his love for her. The devil, on the other hand, used her list of likes to help him become the perfect agent and trick her into choosing him. This is one of the main reasons for unsuccessful relationships: we create our own "perfect agents" while we are dating.

When dating, which is what you do prior to committing to a monogamous relationship, one or both of the individuals involved in this phase of getting to know each other provides the other with many personality likes and dislikes in a possible life partner. But there is a danger in providing people with all your personality likes and dislikes in a potential partner. You are giving this person an opportunity to misuse this information to gain your favor. It's not that I think all people are devilish in their ways. I only mean that people are human beings. Whether good or bad, most people, when given the secret to access what they want, will take those steps to obtain what they want, whether it's with good or bad intent. Sometimes it's unconsciously. So, it's better not to provide your list of personality likes and dislikes at all; that way you actually help those you date to be themselves without being tempted to adjust who they are to try to make you happy or win you over.

Some people aren't happy with themselves, so they try to alter who they are for as long as they can in order to win your heart. There are also people who don't really have a problem with themselves, but they act differently for as long as they can to make you like them. Also, when they become their genuine selves and you point out how they've changed, they resent you for not liking their true selves and accuse you of trying to change them. This is why it's imperative that you not share so much detail about all your personality likes and dislikes. It prevents these types of people from *acting* their way into your heart.

Example 1: While on a dinner date, one might ask the other, "What do you like to do for fun? What do you look for in a man/woman?" Being the nice people that we are, we don't see any harm in answering a question. So we do. We let our date know what kind of man/woman we like, how we like to be treated and talked to, while not missing one detail.

Example 2: While at the beginning stages of dating, without being asked, some people feel they don't want to waste their time, so they lay out their grocery list of likes and dislikes right on the table or, better yet, on their MySpace, Online Dating, or Facebook profiles. They list what they are looking for in a man/woman, and what they will not tolerate.

Example 3: Growing up with a friend of the opposite sex, you may have confided in that friend about the issues in your relationships, not being aware that that person may possibly end up being your mate.

When we freely provide other people with the secrets to our hearts, we are creating our own perfect agents. This is what causes us to be on the phone, talking to this person, thinking and saying, "You are too good to be true!" Well, of course they are, you've told them everything they need to do to effectively seem too good to be true. They paid attention, took mental notes on how to be too good to be true, and duplicated them. Whether people are good or evil, when providing them with this precious information, we put them in a predicament where they have to make a decision on whether they should: a) be themselves, the person that doesn't fit the description of the person we described as our perfect man/woman, or b) do some acting, and live up to those expectations for as long as they can so that they win over the person they are trying to pursue.

A lot of people put in this situation will choose the latter of the two and become an agent. When, or if, someone asks what you look for in a man/woman, you can politely reply, "Time will tell," and hopefully it will be him or her. Let the person know you're not trying to be rude or disrespectful, but you don't want to put anyone in a predicament where they unintentionally alter themselves to try to make you happy. You want them to feel comfortable around you and be themselves.

When in a relationship, it is not your family's or best friend's business. Your relationship is between you and your partner only. You should not be sharing your relationship problems with anyone but the person you are in the relationship with. Sharing intimate information with your best friends or family members gives them the opportunity to give you biased (and terrible) advice. This is another common reason for relationships ending in disaster. We invite third parties into our business and allow them to give us bad advice. We then take this bad advice, as if they are licensed to give it, and our relationships are destroyed.

If you do decide to share relationship information, definitely avoid sharing your intimacy problems with people of the opposite sex who are considered your friend/best friends. You don't know what the future holds. That person may be someone you end up with in the future. It might seem unlikely at that time, but you can't control what your heart may decide in the future. Many relationships begin as friendships. Many also begin as friendships and end as two people despising one another, with the friendship part ended.

I have a friend who was having relationship issues. She didn't go into detail—because I didn't allow her to—but she stated that her man acted a certain way at the beginning "courting" stage of the relationship and changed dramatically once they were a couple. I began to explain that there comes a time in the beginning of new relationships where someone or both parties share their likes and dislikes in a mate, and the other or both parties take mental notes of that and become that person for as long as they can to stay with the mate that they want.

My friend told me that this situation did not apply to her because she never provided him with any information about her likes and dislikes in a relationship. They had only been close friends for a long time before they became an item. I then asked her, "When you were just friends, were you in other relationships?"

She said yes. So I asked her, did she ever share with him any information about the problems she was having in her past relationships, along with the good days?

Though we were conversing on the telephone, she was silent for a minute and I could see the light bulb go off in her head. She replied, "I sure as hell did! I told him everything! I even called him crying sometimes telling him what wrongs the men I was in the relationships with did."

My friend now realized that her giving him all of that information was probably worse than just answering the question of what do you look for in a man, because the way she delivered her secrets to her heart was through passion and emotion. That helped him to know the "must do's" and definite "no no's."

So now you know, "the less you give the more you receive" means the less information you give about what you're looking for in a man/woman, the more you increase your chances of interacting and falling for your potential mate's true self—not their agent. Keep this in mind when in the dating stage, and prevent yourself from creating the perfect agent.

Please don't misunderstand what I'm saying in this chapter in regard to sharing information while dating. I'm speaking solely in regard to personality likes and dislikes as well as physical actions you feel that a male or female should take toward you (i.e., opening doors, complimenting you, being attentive, paying the tab, having manners or table etiquette, being a gentlemen or a lady, etc.). You can feel free to share your favorite hobbies and any other things to help that person know what kind of person you are, such as what you do for fun, types of movies you like, if you like to read or not, whether you like sports or not, etc. Please don't miss the message and become a mute. Just don't share the "recipe" to your love and happiness.

CHAPTER III

———— ✵ ————

Stick to Your Grocery List

Before making the transition from dating to a relationship, or from relationship to marriage, make sure you don't deviate from your grocery list.

You may be wondering, how is making a grocery list going to help me have a better relationship? Picture this: you're at a friend's gathering, and one of the dishes on their menu is macaroni and cheese. You add some to your plate, take a bite, and instantly think to yourself that this is the best macaroni and cheese you have ever tasted in your life. So you immediately run to your friend, after getting seconds and thirds, to say how good it is and ask for the recipe.

Your friend, reluctant to share her kitchen secret for fear that some people don't follow the exact ingredients and end up ruining the recipe, decides to give you the recipe after the party, despite her hesitation. She provides you with the recipe and stresses to you that you not deviate from or alter the recipe. You promise that you won't. Three weekends later, you decide you want some of that wonderful macaroni and cheese. So you take out the recipe and transfer the ingredients from the recipe to a grocery list. You take the list to your favorite grocery store and begin shopping. While strolling down the different aisles, you identify the items from the grocery list, happily grab them, and throw them into your cart. You slowly begin noticing, as you start toward the end of the grocery list, that the store doesn't have all of the items you need. You, being impatient, decide that you aren't going to go from store to store to find the select few items the store was missing. They don't have canned Pet milk, but they do have the Carnation brand, so you buy Carnation milk. They don't have the Breakstone sour cream, but they do have Daisy, so you buy Daisy. Your grocery list had salt on it, and they are out of salt, but you are confident that you have some at home. This decision causes you to break your promise and alter your grocery list.

After completing your shopping for items on your adjusted grocery list, you go to the counter, pay for your items, and head home, excited about the macaroni and cheese you're going to have that night. Upon your arrival home, you begin to cook using your friend's instructions step by step. The first instruction is to bring a pot of two tablespoons of salt, three tablespoons of vegetable oil, and twelve cups of water to a boil. You look in your cabinet for your salt and you're out of salt, so you use seasoning salt instead, and you bring everything else you're supposed to have to a boil. The recipe then says, after bringing those few things to a boil, add the noodles from the Kraft mac and cheese box, and allow them to boil until they are done. You proceed to cook the noodles. The recipe says to drain the noodles, rinse them off, mix two eggs, shred the Cracker Barrel block of cheese, add the rest of the ingredients and mix. When all this is done, set your oven at 425 degrees and bake until cheese on the side is bubbling and the macaroni is golden brown at the top. After the macaroni and cheese fits this description, you take it out of the oven and let it sit for fifteen to twenty minutes to cool down. You then make a plate, take a bite, with the anticipation of tasting the macaroni and cheese you had three weeks ago, but you are extremely disappointed. This macaroni and cheese is disgusting and you can't understand why. Your macaroni and cheese is terrible because you are a human who lives in the time of NOW.

We know what we want and we want it NOW. The only issue is, because of our impatience, even though we know what we want, we alter our mental grocery list, which has the ingredients for our happiness, and we settle for what we have access to at that moment, just to have something a little close to what we want NOW!

While in the dating stages, it is imperative that you take the time to find out and know what is on your grocery list. Your grocery list contains the personality traits you desire in your mate, along with the way you prefer him or her to behave toward you and others. Don't waste your time putting physical features like height, specific hair color or length, weight, light-skinned, dark-skinned, young or old. I can almost guarantee that the person you end up with will be the opposite. Not to mention, with time, most physical appearances change. So if your relationship is based on your mate's physical appearance, time itself will destroy that relationship. Your grocery list, consisting of personality traits and conduct, is the recipe to your happiness. After making this list, *stick to it*.

As I stated, we are humans who live in the time of now, but love and happiness can't be forced or rushed. It is a process. Because we live in the time of now, what tends to happen is, after dating for a while and still not having that special grocery list of a person, we begin to think that maybe our grocery list is asking for too much. We tell ourselves that no one is perfect. Your grocery list is not creating a perfect person; it is creating a person that will make you a happy person. A perfect person is someone who is flawless who can do no wrong and makes everyone happy. That is not realistic; for everyone is different, so no one person can make everyone happy. Also, because everyone's list will be different because people's preferences are different, there is no way your list will contain the features of a "perfect" person. You have a list of values that you are passionate about and, if provided to you, will make you a very happy person. It's when we alter our grocery list and settle for less that our recipe for happiness ends up tasting disgusting.

We begin dating and say to ourselves, "Well, I have a grocery list of fifteen, and he or she has nine of the fifteen items; therefore, he or she must be the one." So you go from dating to a relationship, and guess what the bulk of the issues are in your relationship? The missing groceries! You have problems with the celery, or the cheese he or she is missing, and you're trying to make the person add those to the cart. Relationships and marriages are never perfect. They eventually have some type of complexities. You are taking two different people's mindsets, upbringings, and lifestyles and trying to make them comfortable as one. When beginning a relationship with a person that has missing items from your grocery list, you are beginning a journey that by nature will eventually have hardships, with pre-existing problems.

Had the person in the story of the macaroni and cheese recipe been patient and visited a few more stores to get those select few items that were altered, that person wouldn't have ended up disappointed. The same thing applies when dating. If we are not patient enough to keep dating until we find our complete grocery list in a man or woman, we will continue to put a lot of our heart and valuable time into relationships that will leave us disappointed.

Here are a couple of ways you can find out if the person you are dating matches your grocery list. One way is to ask situational questions that are aligned with the things on your grocery list. For example, if one of the items on your grocery list is to have a man that thinks of men and women as equals, ask how he feels about having a woman president. Another example: one of the ingredients on my grocery list is honesty. I aspired to have a woman who would be honest with me at all times, not just telling me things to please me or make me happy. My reason for this ingredient is I can't grow to become a better person if I'm surrounded by people who aren't honest enough to tell me the truth, even if it hurts, just because they want to make me happy.

During my dating phase, I took a young lady out to dinner, once. Right after we ordered our meals, I asked the young lady if she liked liver with gravy and onions. When I asked this question, I asked in a manner that made it seemed as though I liked liver with gravy and onions. So she said yes, and I replied that I hated liver with gravy and onions. Guess what? She then countered with, "I don't like it, either." So I countered with calling the waiter, telling him that we were no longer interested in eating at their establishment, and I took her home. This may seem harsh to you, but I despise phony people.

One might feel that my approach was deceiving, dishonest, maybe even childish. I must admit, at that time in my life, I was frustrated with females putting up a front to make me like them. I was young, late teens or early twenties, and I did go about that situation immaturely but, at the same time, if someone asks you if one plus one equals two in a manner that seems like it didn't, would you say NO? Then why should it matter how I asked the female the question? If the answer was no, she should have just answered no. I have matured a lot since then and, if I were still single, I wouldn't go about finding out if a female was honest in that manner, but I am glad that I found out she was phony on our first date before investing a lot of time and emotion into a relationship with her.

Another way to find out if a person you are dating matches your grocery list is to be analytical. For example, when on a date, let us say, out to the movies, you realize during the movie that a scenario occurs that aligns with something on your grocery list. This scenario strikes an emotional chord with you, and you're passionate about it because you've had a life experience regarding it, not to mention it's on your grocery list. So you begin to get closer to your date for comfort, and stop because you realize that they think it's humorous. They even elaborate on how funny that scenario was when you two go out to eat after the movie. You then know that that person does not feel the same way you feel about that situation, and clearly is missing that item on your grocery list (whether it be respect, sensitivity, equality, etc.).

I know this example is a little complex, so let me draw a picture to illustrate what I mean. When I was dating my wife, we went to see the movie *Two Can Play That Game* (another ingredient on my grocery list is that I prefer a mature woman who is not petty and vindictive). In the movie, Morris Chestnut played a man who was in love with the character played by Vivica Fox. After he unintentionally hurt her, she intentionally did spiteful things to him, causing him to end the relationship. This caused her to seek further revenge. In one particular scene, she saw him at a party, grabbed a guy that she wasn't really interested in (but she knew he was interested in her) and brought him to meet Morris Chestnut, who she knew still loved her. After introducing the two men, as if the fact that she approached him with another man didn't hurt him enough, she intentionally dropped a condom in front of him and picked it up in a manner that he could see it, and walked off with the other man. Now at this point, I'm uncomfortable in my chair, thinking to myself, *She is so immature, petty, and trifling.* Guess what? My wife, who was my date at the time, said out loud, "She is so trifling!"

I remember smiling, while thinking, *one check for her.* The more we dated, that one check led to all of my grocery items being checked off. I began adding and checking off items on my grocery list, because she provided me with things I hadn't even known I wanted. This led to a serious relationship, which ultimately led to our getting married. If while dating, you refrain from deviating from your grocery list and wait until you find that person who carries all of the ingredients to your grocery list before you begin a serious relationship with someone, the same thing can happen to you.

It is very important that, before you take the next step of going from dating to serious relationship to marriage, you know you are with someone who has all of the items on your grocery list. If you settle for someone with a select few things on your list, the items they are missing, on top of the complexities that already come with a relationship/marriage, are going to be the constant issues that your relationship/marriage will face. Relationships and marriages are huge steps. They come with children, joint accounts, houses, and cars. These are the things you build together when in a relationship/marriage, and if the person you are with doesn't have all the items on your grocery list, you will lack the passion to fight for your relationship/marriage when times get hard. This will cause you to give up on the relationship too easily. The items that the person lacks cause them not to be appealing enough for you to be willing to go through the wilderness with them. This, in turn, causes the relationship/marriage to fail. *Please stick to your grocery list!*

CHAPTER IV

It's Not That They Don't Love You, You Just Don't Love Alike

I find it intriguing that no matter how many weddings I attend, the people, family members, locations, genders, races, situations, cultures, and religions are different, but the advice given remains constant. No matter the wedding, the couple's wedding counselor, friends and family, or both, tell the bride and groom, in their own special way, that the secret to a successful marriage is through communication. If this advice is given, at the least, in every wedding, why is it that, no matter if it's the first, second, or third marriage, one of the top-five reasons for their divorce is lack of communication?

Telling people that the secret to a successful marriage is through communication is too broad a statement. Though communication is a key ingredient to a successful marriage, if you don't know what to communicate about, or the proper way to convey what it is you are trying to say, this advice is useless. This, in turn, can be detrimental to your relationship. Due to this lack of knowledge, many people assume that certain topics aren't important enough to share, so they keep those topics to themselves, causing their mates to think that they don't care about or love them because they don't understand their actions. We assume people will understand us because we often live by the "treat others the way we want to be treated" theory. You might be thinking you treat others the way you want to be treated because that's the way your parents taught you to treat people. Well, I'm apologizing for our parents' bad advice, and I'm here to show you how that advice is the reason that lack of communication is one of the top-five reasons marriages end in divorce.

You are supposed to find out how *your mate wants* to be treated, and treat them as such, not the way *you* want to be treated.

I can see how this may seem contradictory to my previous chapters in the sense that I stated that people tend to act a certain way until they get what they want. But keep in mind that was during the dating phase. I am now referring to the relationship phase, the period after you have found your grocery list of a mate and are willing to make sacrifices to help the *relationship* grow and prosper. So when you have transitioned from the *dating* phase to the *relationship* phase, it's okay to compromise yourself for the sake of the *relationship* growing toward marriage.

The way people think, speak, act, love, worship, treat others, feel, etc., derives solely from what I call a person's "novel." A person's novel is their life's story up to their current self. Their story consists of their childhood, how they were raised, their environment, past relationships, the peers they have or had, the books they've read, the television shows and movies they've watched, situations they've been through that have made a big impact on their lives, the schools they went to, their siblings, etc. All of these things make a person feel, think, act, and love the way they do; so to treat someone the way *you* want to be treated is to assume that their novel is the same as yours. I think we all know what happens when we ASS·U·ME.

It's imperative in a relationship *not* to treat your mate the way you want to be treated. Instead, *seek* to know how *he or she* wants to be treated, and find out *why* your mate prefers to be treated that way, (i.e., find out your mate's novel or story). This will help you understand how important it is to that person, which in turn will help you to remember to treat them in that manner versus the way *you* like to be treated.

Also, since we now know that people tend to treat people the way they like to be treated, it's equally important to pay attention to how your mate treats *you*. The reasons for this are: first, if your mate treats you how he or she likes to be treated, this helps you to know how your mate likes to be treated; second, if the way he or she is treating you is not how you like to be treated, you can help your mate understand that this is not the way to respond to you and explain why (helping your mate to find out more about your novel); third, if after explaining why you would prefer for your mate not to take that approach with you, you ask why he or she responded to you that way, thus you will again learn a little bit more about his or her novel. That's true communication. Let's look at some scenarios to demonstrate what I mean.

This is not an example about a relationship, but it should help wrap your mind around how easily we push our views, which derive from our novels, onto others and judge others when their views don't match ours. This is a very common issue people face in their relationships.

Some have implied that Chinese people eat cats, rats, and mice, and also serve them in their restaurants disguised as other types of meat. I don't know whether it's true or not, but the people I've encountered in my lifetime are passionate about how disgusting this would be. If the subject comes up, whether it's when ordering Chinese food or just having casual conversation, they stress how if they do eat at a Chinese restaurant, they only order shrimp or the other foods that are easily identifiable to them. I laugh and ask them, what makes choosing to eat chicken, fish, beef, shrimp, and the other meats right, and eating cats, rats, and mice wrong? They simply reply with, "It just is."

What these folks really mean is, that's what their novel taught them were the right things to eat. What they fail to realize is, even if this implication about the food in Chinese restaurants is true, it's because that's what their novel taught *them* to eat. In this case, the Chinese people's upbringing or culture was perhaps the part of their novel that may have caused them to feel that eating cats, rats, or mice is the right thing to do. If you were raised in a culture where almost everyone ate rats, cats, and mice on a daily basis, and that's all you knew, you also would feel comfortable eating rats, cats, and mice. Don't judge a book by its cover; read it, and you might understand the reason for the cover.

Now let's analyze the story of Tara and Grant, a married couple with three children who both practice the "treat others the way you like to be treated" theory. Tara is the type of person who, because of her novel, likes to be checked on when she's sick. This simple action shows her that she is cared about and loved. Grant, on the other hand, because of his novel, likes to be left alone when he is sick. It helps him get rest so that he will get better quicker.

One day, Tara became terribly sick, causing her to be bedridden. Her loving husband, Grant, decided (because he hates to be bothered when he is sick, and peace and quiet helps him to rest and get better quicker) to keep out of the room and let Tara rest up so that she could get peace and quiet in an effort to get better quicker. He told the children to do the same.

Poor Tara, she's in bed physically miserable because she's sick, and emotionally miserable (sad) because she feels her husband doesn't care about her since he has yet to come in the room and ask her how she is doing. She feels unloved and is upset with Grant because she feels he is so inconsiderate. She eventually gets well, and Grant thanks the children for helping him get Mom better. Tara never asks Grant why he never checked on her, nor has she told him that she didn't like the fact that he never came to check on her when she was sick. Due to this lack of communication, every time Tara gets sick, the same thing occurs and she resents Grant more and more, thinking he doesn't care, while Grant pats himself on the back, thinking, *another job well done.*

It's now Grant's turn to be sick and bedridden. Tara loves her man, so she wouldn't dare leave him in a room by himself without checking on him. So she frequently visits the bedroom and asks him how he's doing whether he is asleep or not. If he's up, she just asks how he's feeling. If he's asleep, she wakes him up and asks how he's feeling. She also tells the children not to forget to check on their father, or go give him some soup or orange juice.

Poor Grant, it seems like as soon as he begins to achieve REM sleep, someone is waking him to ask him if he's okay or feeling better. Every time he's wakened and asked these questions, he thinks to himself, *I was fine until you woke me up.* He is now angry and decides not to go to sleep at all because he feels he has an inconsiderate family. Grant eventually gets well. Tara thanks the children for helping her nurse Dad back to health. Grant never tells Tara that it irks him to be bothered when he is ill; so every time he's sick, the cycle starts all over again, and he resents Tara who he feels is inconsiderate, while Tara prides herself on not treating him the way he treats her when she's sick.

On the outside looking in, it is obvious to us that Tara and Grant love each other. They just don't love alike. They're both upset with each other for expressing love to one another, or should I say, treating each other the way they each like to be treated themselves. They both decide not to express each other's feelings regarding how they feel they should be treated when they're sick. The reason for this is they both feel it is "common sense" to treat others the way they like to be treated. Again, it's easy to push our novels onto others and judge them because their novel doesn't match ours. Remember the story about the Chinese food?

Now let's analyze a story where communication was practiced. I, due to my novel of life, became a man of detail. This causes me to be very observant. My wife, due to her novel of life, feels that detail is not as important.

At the beginning of my marriage, I would get my hair cut and my beard trimmed and lined up, and my wife never noticed. For years, this frustrated me to no end. Of course, I got my hair cut for myself, but I also kept her in mind. I mean, when we're out in public or I visit her at her job, I represent her just as much as I represent myself. So why not keep myself well groomed? Not to mention, I kept myself groomed before we got married. That's just how I am. Just the thought of me leaving the house looking shabby and coming back home looking like a new man, and her not noticing was enough to make me explode. I had concluded that she didn't care about me. I used to ask myself, *How could you not notice your man's face looks different if you pay him any attention? How could you love someone and not pay them any attention?*

Finally, I got so fed up that I asked her why she didn't pay any attention to me (How could she not notice when I got a haircut? Does she really love me like she says she does? Because her actions sure don't show it according to my novel.).

She simply replied, "Of course, I love you. I can honestly say that I don't notice when you get your hair cut, but your haircut doesn't make you who you are." She said that she loved me for me, not how I look. She stated that if she got excited and noticed when

I got my hair cut that might have suggested that, prior to me getting my hair cut, I didn't look too appealing to her. She helped me realize that she treated me the same at all times, whether I had a haircut or not. I then changed my outlook on how I felt when she didn't notice I got my hair cut. Now I'm happy that she doesn't notice when my hair has been cut. I'm confident that if she does notice when I get a haircut in the future, I'm likely to be furious.

This is definitely a case of me and my wife loving each other, but not loving alike, when I tell her that her nails look nice when she gets them done, or I like how they did her eyes when she gets them arched. This is my way of showing her love by showing her that I am attentive to her.

No matter how unimportant you may think something is, or if you feel that something should be common sense, it's important to communicate how you feel about different situations with your mate and why. The "why" helps your mate identify with your novel, which will help him or her to remember to treat you the way you like to be treated versus the way he or she likes to be treated and vice versa. Because this person is the person who meets your grocery list, you shouldn't mind making this adjustment. This form of communication will help your relationship run much more smoothly and help you to understand your mate better. This will not make you and your mate love alike, but it will help you to understand how to express love to one another.

If Tara had told Grant she liked to be looked in on when she is sick, he would have known to visit the room frequently and ask her how she was feeling, to show her that he is not inconsiderate and that he cares for her and loves her very much. If Grant had told Tara that he likes to be left alone in peace and quiet when he's sick, she would have known to tell the children to stay clear of their father so that he could get his rest, and she would have done the same. This would have prevented Grant from thinking his family was so inconsiderate.

A person's novel plays a critical role on his or her mindset. The power of a person's novel is often overlooked simply because we are overpowered by our own novels or life stories that we are convinced that everyone's outlook on life is the same as ours. This is what causes us to get angry at others if they don't see things the way we see them or come to the same conclusions as we do. A person's novel is so powerful that I've seen it cause a woman who has been mentally, physically, and sexually abused as a child, throughout her teenage years, and most of her adult life, to ruin a relationship with a man who finally treated her as a woman or person should be treated because he *doesn't* mentally, physically, and sexually abuse her. This woman's novel had trained her mind to think the way a man shows he loves her is to mentally, physically, and sexually abuse her. Because of this, when she finally met Mr. Right, she got rid of him because he didn't represent what her novel taught her to seek in regard to love. The man was left confused, wondering what it was that he had done wrong because the life that led the woman to the mental state she was in was never explained.

The proper communication is so vital in a relationship, for it helps a couple to realize that it's not that their mates don't love them; they just don't love alike.

CHAPTER V
―――――― ❧ ――――――

Live, Lie, Steal, Die

I *live* in Chesapeake, Virginia. With high crime and gang violence, it is not uncommon for parents to *live* longer than their children. Because of the Janet Jackson "wardrobe malfunction" incident during the 2004 Super Bowl, the halftime show is no longer *live*. You become more and more untrustworthy every time you tell a *lie*. After a long day's work, I can't wait to go home, take a long hot shower and *lie* down. I'm friends with the owner of the car dealership so I know we can get the car for a *steal*. The young man waited until his parents were asleep to *steal* out of the house to meet his friends at the party. For initiation into the neighborhood gang, the boy had to *steal* a car. We wanted to play Yahtzee, but we were missing a *die*. My friend is always designing something whether it's a scrapbook, greeting cards, decorating bulletin boards, or making table decorations; so I know she'll love this *die*-cutting machine I bought her for Christmas. It pains me to think that a suicide victim's life was so terrible that they wanted to *die*.

Sex in a relationship is just as complicated as the English language. Just like *live, lie, steal,* and *die*, a kiss or any other physical gesture may mean something one day, but mean something totally different the next. This confusing communication barrier often leads to rejection, humiliation, resentment, and frustration in a couple's bedroom. It is common in a relationship for an expression of affection to be misread as an attempt to have sex. This causes the person receiving the gesture of affection to become excited and attempt to take a step further with hopes of having sex. Because the form of affection was not given with the intent of having sex, this tends to lead to rejection for the person trying to have sex. Because of this rejection, the person humiliated and rejected now has a complex and will be hesitant to initiate sex in the future. On the other hand, the person who initiated the gesture that began this snowball effect is now frustrated with his or her mate for misinterpreting their gesture and attempting to make something sexual that they perceived as mere affection. This, whether it leads to the couple having sex or not, can cause the person who just wanted to cuddle, or merely express a mild form of affection, to resent their mate.

Everyone, male and female, aggressive or passive, at some point in time (if not always) craves the feeling of being desired. With this having been said, oftentimes even though we feel the urge to have sex, instead of asking our mate to initiate sex at that moment, we opt to give hints or create temptation in hopes that our mate will be so sexually stimulated by us that they lose control and initiate the sexual act. We opt to take this route because mentally we feel that if they initiate sex with us because we requested it, then it wasn't because they *wanted* or *craved* us, it was something they felt obligated to do, thus negating the sense of us feeling wanted.

The problems derived from these non-verbal hints include: your mate might not catch the hint; or he or she might catch the hint, but because of the complex birthed by rejection in the past they may not attempt to act on it for fear of reading the gesture the wrong way, which could lead to further rejection. Finally, since this is something that *everyone* does, your mate might have the need to feel desired the same time you do, meaning he or she is giving the same hints you are, at the same time, eventuating in neither party taking the bait. No matter which one of these problems presents itself, the end result is always that—at least one person goes to sleep sexually frustrated and upset. I will gladly provide you with a simple solution to this problem after I give you several examples of what I mean.

During a gloomy Saturday while the kids were away, Eric watched his wife Renae as she cleaned and folded clothes and caught up on the taped shows she had missed during the week. After she finished, Eric watched her as she put up her hair, got undressed, and stepped into the shower. He began thinking to himself how beautiful and sexy she was as she massaged lotion into her skin and sprayed herself with perfume, which was her daily routine. He loved that she cared about her fragrance, appearance, and the smoothness of her skin. He grew immediately aroused. When she finished freshening up and getting dressed, Eric hugged and kissed her passionately, followed by a whisper in her ear that he loved her. For the rest of the day, Eric followed his wife's every step throughout the house with his eyes. The more he stared, the more he lusted for her, which led to him again kissing her passionately, but this time following it with the removal of her clothes and guiding her to their bedroom where he showed her what he'd been thinking about all day.

Two weeks later, Eric received a phone call from his best friend Rob who asked him to stop by his place because he needed to talk. Eric told his wife that he would be back because he was going to visit Rob since when he spoke to him something seemed wrong. She acquiesced. Eric gave his wife a kiss, told her he loved her, and left. Upon his arrival, he didn't have to knock on Rob's door, for the door was open with Rob sitting on his living room couch crying.

Eric rushed in and asked what was wrong. He soon learned that Rob had found out that his wife had been cheating on him for several years and that their four-year-old daughter was not his biological child. Eric stayed with Rob for most of the day, with the rest of their friends, trying to show support and lift up his spirits. Eric then headed home to his wife and children, and during the drive began to reflect on his life with his wonderful wife, which filled him with joy and appreciation. Because of this overwhelming appreciation, as soon as Eric saw his wife when he stepped in the house, he hugged and kissed her passionately while whispering in her ear that he appreciated and loved her. This passionate kiss and whisper to the ear mentally brought Eric's wife back to two weeks before when his passionate kiss led to their making love all night. She became aroused and thought to herself, *He doesn't have to tell me twice, he can definitely get some tonight.*

With her arousal and anticipation of how her night was going to end, Eric's wife made sure the children went to bed on time. She showered and put on her best-smelling perfume and lingerie. She crept downstairs to find her husband on the couch with a beer and a bowl of chips mixed with popcorn, watching the Lakers game. Though she found what he was doing to be odd because of the obvious hinted gesture that was given to her earlier in the evening, she attempted to get something started anyway by kissing on his neck. Because Eric was into the game, with sex far from his mind, he moved away and told Renae, "Not tonight."

Two weeks later, Renae was beginning to prepare dinner so that Eric would have something to eat when he got home. This was one of the weekends that he had to work. Eric finally arrived home with two-dozen roses and some cards for Renae, "just because." This was something he did frequently enough to say he always did it, but sporadically enough for it to be a surprise. She loved it. As she began reading her cards, he went straight to his children, asking them what they had done that day. This led to him helping his daughter with the homework that she told him she was having difficulty with. As Renae was cooking in the kitchen, she couldn't help but frequent the dining room to watch Eric as he effortlessly interacted with the children and resolved their needs and problems after a long day's work. She finally finished preparing the meal and told everyone that dinner was ready. Everyone washed their hands and met at the table where dinner was served. As they began to eat, Eric asked his wife what her day consisted of. She loved how he was always so interested in what was going on with her and the family. After dinner, it was almost time for the family's favorite show to come on so everybody put their dishes in the dishwasher and met in the living room to watch TV.

After the show was over, it was time for the kids to start getting ready for bed. While they were doing that, Eric used that time to get in his daily exercise so that he could shower after they were done. With every curl of his dumbbell, every crunch of his stomach, and every push-up he completed, Renae watched. She watched and thought to herself how lucky she was to have such a well-rounded man, a man that helps with the children, is interested in their family, works hard, and takes care of his and her bodies. This thought made her aroused and determined to show her appreciation in a physical manner. She smiled as she thought to herself that they didn't have ice cream, but he was getting dessert tonight.

While the children were all in their beds after saying their goodnights, Eric headed upstairs to get in the shower to wash off the long day's work and the evening exercise. As he took his shower, he was surprised to see that he was accompanied by Renae. They talked and washed each other's bodies. After the shower, she massaged lotion into her skin, sprayed her perfume, and they met each other in the bed. They lay on their sides chest to chest and told each other that they loved one another. Renae leaned in and gave him a passionate kiss, turned around and scooted her behind against him, and placed his hands on her breast. This was how she began to give him his dessert of appreciation.

During a freezing day in mid-January, Eric and Renae decided to have friends over for a game night. Eric was in charge of the chili and hot wings, while Renae whipped up her well-known dips. All of their friends slowly began to arrive around seven p.m. From then until one a.m. everyone laughed, sang, ate, and played board games. When the game night ended, Eric and Renae escorted each one of their friends to their cars and began cleaning up their house. They cleaned up the kitchen and living room together while laughing about the highlights of the evening.

They shared a steaming hot shower, because Renae stressed that her body was freezing. After the shower, Renae massaged her lotion in her skin, sprayed herself with perfume, and joined Eric in the bed. Because she was still cold she hurried under the covers, kissed Eric, turned around and scooted her behind and back against him, and pulled his arms around her for warmth and comfort. This maneuver reminded Eric of the night she gave him that amazing dessert of appreciation, causing him to get aroused. He moved his arms from a comforting holding position to placing his hand on her breast. Renae scooted away from him and told him she was tired— "not tonight."

The next day the kids were still gone for the weekend. Renae remembered what happened the night before and was feeling a little horny with the hopes that Eric would attempt to get some again, because he could definitely get some this day. Eric was still sexually worked up from yesterday, but this was one of the days that he needed to feel desired and hoped that with just the right amount of temptation, Renae would become aroused enough to pursue him and initiate what was always some good sex. The day was full of coincidental touches and grazing against each other's bodies when they crossed paths. Though it was the coldest month of the winter, Eric walked around in just his boxers, which consisted of a bulge because he was aroused all day.

Renae walked around the house in her see-through lingerie and made sure she had a lot to pick up around Eric to show she wasn't wearing any panties—as if Eric couldn't tell she wasn't wearing any panties with the see-through lingerie she was wearing. The whole day they were competing for the same thing and didn't know it. The day finally ended with them taking a shower together, Renae massaging lotion into her skin, and spraying perfume all over her body. Consequently, both of them met in bed with no clothes or undergarments. They were in their bed chest to chest giving each other the bedroom eyes, conversing about their weekend with interjections of "I love you" in the middle of each other's conversation. Eric leaned in and kissed Renae on the forehead; she turned around and scooted her behind against Eric's manhood. Eric, who was already aroused, made his girth pulsate against her behind to signal to her that he was horny. Renae shifted her hips left and right, moving her behind against his genitalia to show him that she felt the same. This continued for the next fifteen minutes, leaving Eric thinking, *why won't Renae turn around and get this thing started?*

Renae wondered why Eric wouldn't grab her breast, kiss and rub on her, or something, since she clearly was showing him that she wanted some. After fifteen minutes of confusion, which turned to frustration, Eric finally turned his back to Renae and slammed his head on his pillow in frustration because he was extremely horny, but concluded that she wasn't going to take the bait.

Renae, whose back was already turned to Eric, just adjusted her pillow for comfort and rolled her eyes, thinking how slow Eric was for not being able to get the hint. They ended up sexually frustrated because they both craved the sense of feeling desired at the same time and didn't know it.

This seemingly complex situation can be simplified by devising a special symbol or sign that helps you and your mate know that, when this sign or symbol is visible, the person who put it there is either open to further intimacy or wants to be seduced. This subtle form of communication can eliminate a great deal of rejection, humiliation, resentment, and frustration from a couple's sex life.

For example, say the sign or symbol Eric and Renae came up with was a scarf on the door knob of the bathroom connected to their bedroom. The night Eric got aroused when his wife wanted to cuddle and use his body for warmth and comfort, he would have realized that the scarf was not on the door and known not to attempt to have sex with Renae because, without the scarf on the door, the gesture was clearly not with the intent of having sex. This would have kept Eric from being rejected, and kept Renae from being frustrated by his taking her mild desire of affection and warmth the wrong way.

This symbol can also avoid nights of pointless hints that lead to frustration (and no sex). If the scarf isn't on the door there is no reason to think either of you desire to have sex. On the other hand, if the scarf is on the door, and you know you didn't put it there, any gesture given by your mate is with the clear intent of having sex. Not to mention if you see that your mate put the scarf on the door, and you know this is not a good time, you should take the scarf or symbol down immediately and explain to your mate why tonight is not a good night, whether it's because you're tired, not feeling well, prefer to watch TV, or any of a million possible reasons. This is much better than your mate giving all of these subtle hints through the night, thinking the hints are working, getting excited, only to find that when the attempt to have sex is made, he or she is rejected.

On nights where you both are having that moment where you need to feel desired, and the other person puts the scarf on the door knob before you, find another scarf and put it on top of the first scarf, or take heart in the knowledge that the scarf is a clear indicator that you are desired and savor the moment. Then you both can find a way to fulfill each other's needs.

If you find that you are always the passive person in the bedroom, bear in mind that your mate needs to feel desired as well. Take note when your mate expresses this, whether verbal or non-verbal. If this behavior goes uncorrected, you may create a climate for your mate to seek that fulfillment elsewhere. I assure you, if a person expresses that need to be desired—especially if it's verbally—and you fail to address that need, they will ultimately fill that void by some means. This is when you will find that your mate no longer attempts to initiate sex with you anymore because they have grown frustrated with the one-sided nature of bedroom antics and found another way to fill their void—whether it's by themselves or with someone else.

In the end, non-verbal communication can be just as effective as verbal communication when used correctly. Even though the English language is complicated, when words like *live, lie, steal,* and *die* are surrounded by other words in a sentence, it makes it easier to understand what they mean. Coming up with an indicator for you and your mate will serve as your surrounding words to a sentence filled with words like *live, lie, steal,* or *die.* So now you have some indication as to why some of your hints did not lead to the desired reply. It's because you didn't understand *live, lie, steal,* or *die.*

CHAPTER VI

———— ༄ ————

Are You For Change or the Same?

"The best time to prevent divorce is before marriage."

J. Murphy (2008)

Another common form of miscommunication that's detrimental to relationships occurs during a couple's transition from relationship to marriage. I am convinced that outside of arranged marriages, people get married for one of two reasons: they're currently happy with how their existing relationship has been going and they can see themselves having that type of relationship for the rest of their lives (same), or they have a mental picture of what marriage is supposed to be like and, though it doesn't match what has been going on in their current relationship, they think that that picture will come into focus after they say, "I do!" (change). No matter which of the two reasons a person chooses to get married, the choice forms a mental picture in that person's mind of what married life will be with their mate. That mental depiction will be aligned with the reason that the person chose to get married, and that will be the life this person expects to come to fruition after he or she says, "I do."

The problem with this situation is that it's very common for the couple's reasons for getting married not to match. Not knowing this, because it was not communicated by either party prior to the couple getting married, causes conflict in the marriage because they're both expecting the mental pictures each person (individually) created about the marriage to come to life.

As human beings, we are blessed by a higher being with

the gift to bring whatever we envision to life. As soon as our minds birth an idea or desire that doesn't match what we have before us, we become uneasy and become inventors, thus inventing ways to breathe life into our ideas and desires. This is a system that we acquire at birth, tweak throughout our childhood and perfect by the time we are adults. As infants we learn that when we cry, we will be picked up, have our diapers changed, receive nourishment, or otherwise gain attention. As children, if denied money for a Popsicle, we might begin looking in the couch for change or become even more resourceful by putting some sweet Kool-Aid in a plastic cup and freezing it, creating our own ICEE. As adults, there might have been a time when we've said to ourselves, "If I could just make it through this week, I'd be okay…" only to find ourselves saying the same thing to ourselves months or even years later because we figured out a way to make it through the week that we had once hoped to make it through. All of our lives we've been accustomed to manifesting our visions. The challenge with this, as it pertains to marriage, comes when your mental depiction of marriage doesn't match your partner's. The challenge would be that you're now sharing *one* life, but trying to manifest *two* diverse visions. Here are a few stories to help you understand what I mean.

Justine, a non-confrontational woman who has strong family values and is married to Dwayne, a hardworking man who feels that as long as he's the provider he should be able to do whatever he wants without being questioned. They were in a relationship for five years before their two-year marriage. During this seven-year span, they lived together for five years and have three children. Prior to popping the big question, Dwayne often spent time with his male friends arriving home early in the a.m., and he never spent much time with his children. When he did come home from work, he had a hot meal and a clean house waiting for him. He spent a lot of time playing Play Station and texting people on his cell phone. He never helped with the household duties and spent time with Justine when *he* wanted to.

When listening to his friends' complaints about their girlfriends or wives, he laughed and said he didn't have to deal with the mess they were going through. They envied him and he loved it. He was the man in his eyes and in theirs. This was his life for five years without one complaint from Justine. So deciding to pop the big question to Justine was the easiest decision Dwayne felt he ever had to make in his life. He had no problems living the life he had been living for the past four-and-a-half years, for the rest of his life. He felt like a king in his home. He thought about the fact that he never got any lip from his woman about where he was, why he never helped around the house, why he never spent time with her and the kids, why he was always playing his games, etc., and decided to ask her to marry him.

She happily said yes, but when she said yes, her vision of what married life was going to be like was totally different from Dwayne's. She was relieved that the mental portrait of marriage she'd drawn was finally going to be unveiled in her life. She was so happy that Dwayne was soon going to spend more quality time with her and the children, that he was going to begin complimenting her and helping around the house. She loved the idea that he was going to be coming home at a reasonable hour daily to be home with the family. She couldn't wait to pack up the Play Station she had been competing with for all those years and give it to the kids. Justine was happy to say yes. She was well on her way to being appreciated and having a partner instead of a headache. They both were so excited about getting married that neither one of them got cold feet before the wedding.

The wedding was beautiful. They both looked and seemed so happy with each other. It might have had something to do with the future that they mentally created for themselves. Those who attended and viewed the couple at the wedding felt that it was clearly a marriage that would last forever.

Two weeks went by; they were finally settled in at home as Mr. and Mrs. Dwayne Miller. That Monday, Dwayne went back to work and decided to hang out with the guys after work and catch up. Justine realized at seven p.m. that Dwayne had been off for two hours and hadn't been home yet. She decided to call his cell phone. Dwayne, while playing pool with the guys, got the phone call, looked surprised when he saw that it was Justine, and answered. She asked where he was and he told her—at the bar playing pool with his friends. She asked him why he didn't call and let her know that was what he was doing after he got off work. He looked around at his BOYS who were looking at him, smiling.

Because he was embarrassed, he got mad and replied, "Because I never did it before so I'm not going to start now," and hung up the phone. She called him back several times and he didn't answer the phone. His friends teased him about the situation, which made him angrier and caused him to go home adamant about rectifying the situation.

Dwayne arrived home to find that Justine had the same intentions. They argued each other's points, yelling and screaming. His point was she never reacted like this before when he went out after work. Her point was that he was inconsiderate and that he should have called and discussed what he was doing after work with her. This was the beginning of their fighting for their mental pictures of marriage to come to life. Dwayne soon found out, through many arguments, that Justine had a problem with him not spending time with her and the children. She didn't like the fact that he always played Play Station and hung out with the guys. She wanted help around the house and expected him home after work daily. They were both frustrated and confused. Their mental pictures of marriage weren't matching their actual marriage. This caused them to resent each other, which caused them to have more bad days than good days, and eventually the marriage ended in divorce.

Let's take a look at the life of Trina and Marcus. Marcus is a successful family-oriented man raised in a single-parent home with his mother and four older sisters. Due to Marcus's father abandoning him and his sisters at such a young age, their mother was adamant about her children being independent and not relying on anyone. She made sure they all knew how to cook, clean, manage their own money, and keep up with their chores to instill a high-quality work ethic. This made the transition from childhood to being adults on their own in the workplace very smooth for Marcus and his siblings. Marcus's upbringing also birthed a vision of what type of wife he wanted to have. He wanted a wife who knew how to cook, kept her house clean, did well with money, and could maintain the household for their future children if/when he passed away.

Trina was also a family-oriented child with a single parent, mother, and siblings. Her siblings were brothers, and she was also the youngest. Trina always had money because her mother always gave it to her. Her room, along with her mother's house, was always clean because her mother kept it clean. Trina and her brothers didn't know how to cook because their mother always cooked for them. Every weekend when Marcus visited Trina while they were dating, he always saw her mother washing and folding her and her brothers' clothes. Marcus admired how Trina's mother was so strong and versatile, and concluded that since Trina looked just like her mother, and was raised by her, she would be similar to her mother as a wife. Like mother like daughter, right?

Wrong. Marcus disregarded the fact that he never saw Trina cook, clean, keep up, either her room or her mother's house, during their entire relationship prior to their marriage. He saw his dream wife in Trina's mother with the assumption that Trina would adopt those qualities and transfer them into their household when they were married.

Trina, on the other hand, enjoyed the fact that she had a man that could cook, clean, had good credit, and kept a great job. She always wanted a man that would be able to take care of her. She admired Marcus's willingness to work hard, cook, clean, pay his bills, and pamper her. She loved how he accepted her for her, and never tried to change her. She was no cook, she never had a job, and her mom teased her and said she was lazy; but she didn't care. She was fine with how she was, and felt that she would just have to find a man that accepted her for who she was. She thought she did in Marcus, until they began their marriage.

After their beautiful wedding and smooth transition into their new home, Marcus and Trina immediately began having problems. Trina wasn't cleaning up after herself, and she never had dinner ready when Marcus came home. She let clothes pile up, and didn't even put dirty dishes in the dishwasher. Trina lived in her new home the same way she lived in her mother's home, minus the maid—her mother.

Though Trina never gave Marcus any reason for him to feel she was anything like her mother, the fact that she wasn't anything like her mother caused Marcus to resent her, feeling that this was not what he signed up for. He began complaining and fussing at Trina for not being domestically inclined, and at least having his dinner ready after he came home from a long day's work. He felt unappreciated and hated the fact that after getting off from work he had to come home to more work. His fussing and complaining at Trina led to arguments because Trina wasn't doing anything different from what she had been doing since they'd been together.

Her argument was that she didn't even cook and clean for her mother, so why would he expect her to do those things for him? Her mother worked, too, and didn't expect half the things he was expecting. So mentally, this wasn't what Trina signed up for either. These two have now begun to battle for each other's mental pictures of what marriage is supposed to be, not realizing that the only way for them to win this battle is for them to share the same mental picture because they are now one person.

Let me introduce you to Trent and Jasmine. Jasmine is a beautiful, domestically inclined, hard-working, educated woman with a slight self-esteem problem. She's a very loving and caring person who aspires to heal the world. People really respond to Jasmine and she gets along with everyone. It's weird because she's married to Trent who's been abusive since three months into their relationship three years ago.

When Trent and Jasmine were dating, he abused her mentally and physically. He dictated what she wore, who she hung out with, when she ate, what she ate, and how she spoke. Trent started off beating Jasmine and apologizing, stating that he would never beat her again. After repeatedly taking him back, the apologies disappeared, and the beatings kept coming. She became an artist with her beauty supplies in a very short period of time, while dating Trent. (She had to hide the bruises.) Trent finally proposed, which translated to *change* in Jasmine's mind, causing her to say "yes" happily. Unfortunately, Trent had no intentions of changing (*same*), eventually causing "death do them part" two months after their wedding.

Sometimes both parties get married for *change*, like Patrick and Cynthia. Cynthia and Patrick dated and tried the relationship thing on and off for seven years. They broke up several times for many different reasons. Once it was because Patrick cheated on Cynthia. Then it was because Cynthia cheated on Patrick. The other times were because they didn't get along and they had different views of life; their families didn't like them together, they didn't trust each other and, lastly, they agreed they weren't compatible. They might have stayed separated and moved on with their lives this time if Cynthia hadn't become pregnant, but she did.

This situation helped them realize that they both had something in common: they didn't want to bring a baby into the world without both parents to raise it. So they decided to get married *(change)*. They both agreed that raising a baby with both mother and father in the household would be the best thing for their child. They assumed that *changing* their status from single to married would help to raise a better child, disregarding the fact that they weren't compatible, didn't trust or like each other, and clearly had different views of life.

Sadly enough, the baby was raised with the opposite outcome of their aspirations. All they did was fight and argue over the same things they broke up for in the past. Only this time it was in front of their baby. This was done throughout their son's childhood, and topped off with a divorce by the time the child was nine. This behavior, along with the divorce, damaged the child emotionally, causing the child to grow up recycling what Mom and Dad did in their relationship in his relationships. Sadly, the baby never had a chance to see how good Mom and Dad treated each other when they were apart, or even how they might have treated someone else that they really liked and loved if they had stuck with their decision to move on. The child probably would have grown to have better communication skills and a better understanding of how to show people loving and caring behavior.

Though not all marriages created under false pretenses end in divorce, it's a much smoother experience when the couple gets married with the *same* perception of what marriage is. When a couple gets married with the *same* idea of marriage in mind, the probability of the union being successful is much greater than a couple with different agendas. Such is the story of Allen and Patricia.

Allen and Patricia make a beautiful couple. They met in college with no intention of being an item. Allen saw Patricia daily in the student union building, sleeping on the couch. He nudged her out of her sleep daily, teasing her about how she knew she had school that day, so she had no business staying up so late the night before. He did this for a while until he found out why she was so tired every day. She was a full-time student with a one-year-old boy at home who kept her up all night. This caused Allen to look at her differently, for he always knew he wanted a woman who was good with children, who had goals and drive. The fact that she was a single parent that did not allow her child to stop her from setting goals and getting an education was very attractive to Allen. These were important items on his *grocery list*. Needless to say, after finding out about the baby at home, Allen let Patricia sleep whenever he saw her in the student union. Allen made sure he attended any event he knew Patricia would be attending. He called her on Mother's Day and always made it known that he was available if she needed him. They soon began dating.

Patricia enjoyed the dating phase of their life. Because she was very protective of her child, it took awhile for her to introduce her son to Allen. After several dates, she realized that he was a respectful gentleman with great morals and values. She loved how he interacted with his mother and family, and he had a big heart for people. These actions finally helped her to decide to let him meet her now two-year-old son. He immediately fell in love with her son and treated him as if he were his own, putting the child's best interests in mind with every decision he made. Patricia loved the fact that Allen loved to cook, and he was "domesticated," especially since she didn't know her way around the kitchen. They just seemed to complement each other so well. Where one was weak, the other was strong; they brought balance into each other's lives.

Six months into bumping their dating status to a relationship, Allen analyzed the year he and Patricia had known each other and the six months that they were in a relationship, and decided that the way life has been with them as a unit—him, her, and her son—was a life he wanted to make permanent. Six months later, he asked Patricia to marry him. She happily said, "Yes!" while thinking to herself that she could see her son and herself living the way she'd been living that past year and a half. With no change expected from either Patricia or Allen, outside of their two planned added members to the family, they had a smooth transition from a relationship to a successful marriage.

I'm confident that many are convinced that their selected reason for getting married, whether it's for *change* or the *same*, is the common sense or correct reason for anyone to want to get married. Most people are overpowered by their novel, causing them to think others view things the way they do, remember? Neither reason, whether it be getting married for *change* or the *same,* is right or wrong. Those who get married for the *same* may argue that it makes no sense to think that if you're in a relationship for a certain period of time and things have been going a certain way that after you say, "I do!" that those things are going to change. By the same token, people who get married for *change* may argue that people's perceptions are their realities. These are both very true statements.

In the end, the most important thing is to communicate your reason for wanting to be married, prior to making this lifelong commitment, to ensure a smoother transition on your journey as husband and wife. This will give you and your mate a chance to clear up any ambiguity as to the intent of your passion for wanting to be married. You may find that your mate has change in mind for you, and assumes that this change will come when you're married. On the other hand, your mate may be so happy with whom and how you are, that they want to marry you before someone else steals your interest. Everything happens for a reason, and marriage is the worst time for a couple's reasons to be opposite. Communicating your reasons for wanting to get married to your mate will birth the opportunity to reduce the chances of your marriage being filled with resentment and hate.

CHAPTER VII

Remain the Same and Lose the Flame

Any person blessed with the ability to hear has had or has a favorite song, a song that was so well put together that when you heard it you had to have a copy so you could play it over and over and over again. Finally, when you purchased the album, you did just that. You blasted the song at your house, on your stereo, walkman, mp3 player, or iPod. Sometimes while blasting the song in your car, you were a few minutes late clocking in to work, because you had to finish the whole song before exiting the ride. Let your friends and family tell it, you played the song to death and they were tired of hearing it. This didn't stop you though; you just kept on playing it, even on repeat. You knew everything about the song; you even sang the adlibs. You couldn't get over how everything was so well put together…how the person who sings the song was chosen, the way the music came in on certain parts, the types of instruments used for the song, how the song related to how you were feeling during that time of your life, how the song took you mentally to a different place from where you were and, of course, the breakdown part of the song that you just couldn't get enough of.

Now even though this was such an incredible song, and it made you feel so wonderful when you heard it for such a long period of time, you eventually stopped playing it. The reason for this is you spent a whole lot of time with a song that never changed. You knew everything the song was going to say before it was said, how the instruments were going to come in before they came in, the message of the song, and how the breakdown part was going to begin and end before it arrived in the song. The song was repetitive and never changed, causing it no longer to be intriguing. This is a very common issue plaguing relationships and marriages.

For example, any sexually active person will agree that they have had sex with someone where the sex was great in the beginning and it grew to be lackluster or lame. One of three possibilities caused this to happen: either you stopped growing as a person, your mate stopped growing as a person, or both of you stunted your growth.

Just like your favorite song, both of you were intriguing to one another in the beginning. You didn't know everything about each other and were mysterious to one another during the dating and relationship stages. This brought about mental stimulation, making the sex amazing. As time passed, the two of you spent a lot of time together physically, on the phone or living together, and eventually you were no longer mysterious or intriguing. You began to know what he or she was going to say before saying it, knew how sex was going to start and how it was going to end, knew all his or her likes and dislikes, had nothing new to talk about and knew exactly what they were going to do when they arrived in your presence.

This experience wasn't like the favorite song though; you couldn't just stop listening to it because it grew boring with no surprise. This was a human being and, because they didn't grow and became stagnant in their personal development, you had nothing new to learn about them and you had to just deal with them playing their same song unless you broke up with or divorced them.

In my opinion, satisfaction derived from sex, relationships, and marriage is ninety percent mental and ten percent physical. This is why a male may have difficulty getting an erection and a non-menopausal woman may have difficulty producing vaginal lubricants when attempting to engage in sex. The mind makes the body and, if you're not mentally aroused by your mate anymore, your body and body language will express this reality.

Whether single, in a committed relationship, or married, it's in a person's best interest not to ever get comfortable with who they are or where they are in life. You can always do better than your current situation and be better than your current self. In reference to relationships and marriages, the secret to keeping them new and intriguing is keeping yourself new and intriguing to your mate. This can be accomplished by consistently self-improving, not necessarily liking your mate's passions, but being well versed or educated about them and challenging yourself to stay innovative.

Self-improvement is improvement of one's condition through one's own efforts. This can be improvement of your character, spirituality, mentality, financial education, political knowledge, health, athleticism, cooking skills, parenting skills, etc. There is an infinite amount of things you can improve when it comes to self. Self-improvement can be attained by reading or listening to books, attending lectures or retreats, spending time with people who know more than you, or, if need be, changing who your friends are because you are more than likely a reflection of who you hang out with, or simply forcing yourself to be a better listener, just to name a few. Self-improvement puts you in a win-win situation. On one hand, you continue to become a better and well-versed person and, on the other hand, your continuous growth in character and mentality will keep your mate mentally intrigued and stimulated by the constant newness you bring to your relationship or marriage.

It is imperative that you become, if you are not already, educated and well-versed in whatever your mate's passion or passions are. I'm not saying you have to like it or them, but it would behoove you to be versed enough to be able to articulate why you don't enjoy his or her passions. This is a very powerful conversational piece as well as a way of showing support. You're more interesting to your mate if the two of you can converse or even debate about what's going on with their passion.

For example, at the beginning of my marriage, I began to realize that my wife and I didn't spend much time with each other after work. Our normal routine was that I came home from work and began cooking. My wife was either watching whatever TV shows she previously recorded that day, or surfing the Internet. When I finished cooking dinner, my family and I found out how everyone's day was. After dinner, depending on if my wife went back to her previously recorded shows or surfing the Internet, I read, used the computer, or found a re-run of an old show that I used to watch growing up. This usually lasted until about ten-thirty p.m., when my wife and I showered together and were in bed by eleven.

After noticing this was a continuous routine, I began to analyze my wife to understand what it was that held her attention five days a week on the Internet and the television. Surprisingly enough, it was the same thing for both, and when she was on the phone speaking with her mom on those days, she was speaking about the same thing she was reading on the Internet and recording on television. My wife's passion was *General Hospital*.

Now I'm not big on television, let alone soap operas, but since *General Hospital* was winning so much of my wife's attention, I wanted to know what the big deal was. So I began watching it with her. At first, mentally I was going about watching *General Hospital* in an ignorant way, telling myself I'm not going to like it because soaps are for *WOMEN*, not to mention a pet peeve of mine is wasting time because you can't get it back. Little did I know that the forty-five minutes of what I thought to be invaluable time would add endless hours of fun and happiness to my marriage. My wife and I had debates about the different episodes. Though they were debates, we were interacting about something she was passionate about so it wasn't a bad thing. We joked about how dumb some of the characters were to us; we formed our own inside jokes that related to the show that no one understood but us when we were out; we set a time every day that was for us to watch *General Hospital* with no interruptions. I now have it so bad that I know all the characters by name and get angry because I have to wait an entire week just for one situation to unravel. Anyone who watches soaps knows what I'm talking about. My seeking and educating myself about my wife's passion created a bond and a friendship within a friendship, as well as motivating my wife to seek and educate herself about my passions, for she now sets aside time to watch and do the things I'm passionate about.

Being innovative is something small, yet so big. Repetitiveness is great for learning, but in a relationship or marriage, it can be grounds for an argument. Even if you do something that's considered nice, if it's repetitive it can be detrimental. It's okay to even keep the same idea, but switch it up a little bit to add surprise and newness. For example, if you always send your spouse roses to his or her job, send a cake next with the inscription, "Celebrating You Just Because." If you always send text messages to your mate throughout the day, send a media message where they can see a video recording of what you want to say. If your spouse is usually the aggressor when it comes to sex, reverse roles next time and make the overture. If you and your family dine at the same restaurant all of the time, make it your duty to seek new restaurants as much as you can. There are also things you can do together that are repetitive, yet always new, such as reading different books together or going to the movies. Outside of keeping yourself interesting to your spouse, being innovative expresses thoughtfulness, consideration, and appreciation to your loved one. It is very difficult to be replaced when you master the art of innovation.

It's imperative to bring as much newness as you can to your relationship or marriage, whether it is mental or physical, to keep yourself continuing to become a new song. This will be no easy task, for no journey to success is. But if you dedicate yourself to the journey, you will find nothing short of happiness.

Do what most people don't do, to have what most people don't have.

This is simply relationship awareness meant to unveil the small, yet big, issues that we overlook during the transition from dating, to a new relationship and, finally, marriage. The intent is to help reveal relationship mistakes we've made in our past while helping to prevent us from making regrettable mistakes in the future. The goal will not be met by simply reading this book once. This is my reason for titling it *The **Handbook** for Increasing Your Relationship IQ*. It's written in a manner that makes it easy for you to refer to the chapter that relates to your current situation. As stated in the beginning of this book, forty-to-fifty percent of first-time and sixty-to-seventy percent of second and third marriages end in divorce. The wisdom in this book will empower you to decrease the odds of becoming one of these statistics.

ACKNOWLEDGEMENTS

—— ৵ ——

I first thank God for the gifts of perspective, creativity, and the ability to convey important messages.

To my lovely wife, Zanetta, I appreciate your honesty and patience during our experimental journey toward increasing our relationship IQ. Because of you I have learned many lessons about love and life—and hopefully I've managed to share some of them in this book. I love you.

I thank Ms. Mahogany Vaughn for pushing me to put my thoughts into book form to expand the circle of people that my gift is shared with.

I thank my father, Pastor Edward Fairley, for challenging me intellectually and inspiring me to creatively touch the lives of others.

I thank a very dear friend, one who I consider a long lost brother who drives and motivates me to do and be better: Jermaine Lewis.

Lastly, to every person that has read this book during the creating process and provided me with honest and genuine feedback, I thank you.

ABOUT THE AUTHOR

———— ❦ ————

Edward Fairley considers himself a spiritual individual who believes he was created to help people gain the knowledge he wishes he attained much earlier in life, by teaching and inspiring in a manner that makes possible the transformation of the negatives in life to positives. He is an advertising executive for the *Virginian-Pilot*.

He enjoys his wife and two children, public speaking, mentoring, reading, cooking, stepping, and participating in a plethora of other self-improvement pursuits.

RESOURCES

Grazian, R. (2008, September 4). "Statistics of Divorce" Retrieved
September 9, 2009, from http://ezinearticles.com/?Statistics-of-
Divorce&id=1468444

Murphy, J., *The Power of Your Subconscious Mind.* Penguin Group
USA, Inc. New York, New York, 2008.